Scary Creatures
of the
NIGHT

Written by
John Malam

Created and designed
by David Salariya

BOOK HOUSE

Long-eared owl

Author:

John Malam studied ancient history and archaeology at the University of Birmingham, England, after which he worked as an archaeologist at the Ironbridge Gorge Museum in Shropshire. He is now an author specialising in information books for children on a wide range of subjects. He lives in Cheshire with his wife and their two young children. Website: www.johnmalam.co.uk

Artists:

John Francis
Robert Morton
Carolyn Scrace
Bob Hersey
Lizzie Harper
Mark Bergin

Series Creator:

David Salariya was born in Dundee, Scotland. In 1989 he established The Salariya Book Company. He has illustrated a wide range of books and has created many new series for publishers in the UK and overseas. He lives in Brighton with his wife, illustrator Shirley Willis, and their son.

Editor: Stephen Haynes

Editorial Assistants:
Rob Walker, Tanya Kant

Picture Research:
Mark Bergin, Carolyn Franklin

Photo Credits:

ANT Photo Library/NHPA: 9
Cadmium: 10, 14, 22, 23
Gerry Cambridge/NHPA: 29
Corbis: 5
Ingram Publishing: 24
John Foxx Images: 11

Published in Great Britain in 2008 by Book House, an imprint of **The Salariya Book Company Ltd** 25 Marlborough Place, Brighton BN1 1UB

SALARIYA

A catalogue record for this book is available from the British Library.

HB ISBN: 978-1-905638-91-8
PB ISBN: 978-1-905638-92-5

Printed in China

PAPER FROM SUSTAINABLE FORESTS

Visit our website at **www.book-house.co.uk** for *free* electronic versions of:
You Wouldn't Want to be an Egyptian Mummy!
You Wouldn't Want to be a Roman Gladiator!
Avoid Joining Shackleton's Polar Expedition!
Avoid Sailing on a 19th-Century Whaling Ship!

Contents

Three-toed sloth

Mouse opossum

Owl monkey

Hawk moth

Olingo

Silky anteater

Red-eyed tree frog

4

What are night creatures?

When the sun goes down, it's time for many animals to wake up. As daylight fades, out come bats, boa constrictors, spiders, owls, and many more. These are **nocturnal** animals: they sleep in the day and become active at night. Darkness is when these animals see best, feed best and stay safest. Nocturnal animals have learnt to live in the dark, and they have developed ways of making the most of the night-time.

Most owls are night hunters. They have big eyes that are extremely sensitive to light. An owl can see its **prey** in very low light, and swoop down quickly and quietly.

 Did You Know?

Guinea pigs, rabbits, foxes, moths and beetles are called **crepuscular** (twilight) animals. They are active at dawn, before it is too light, and at dusk, before it is too dark.

Many nocturnal animals, from tiny frogs to large mammals, live in the **tropical** rainforest of South America. The picture opposite shows just a few of them.

A boa constrictor can open its jaws very wide to swallow an animal bigger than its own head. Its sharp teeth drag the prey into its throat, and as the snake swallows, its meal slides down into its stomach.

Boa constrictor

X-Ray Vision

Hold the next page up to the light to see what's inside a boa constrictor.

See what's inside

Are boa constrictors strong?

Yes! Boa constrictors are big, strong snakes that live in the deserts, grasslands and forests of South and Central America. They live on the ground and in trees, and they hunt at night. Boas eat lizards, bats, birds, rats, monkeys and squirrels, which they kill by **constriction**. They twist tightly around their prey, crush them to death, then swallow their bodies whole, head first.

Full stomach

Monkey inside the boa constrictor's stomach

What do night animals do in the day?

After being awake and active during the night, nocturnal animals use the daytime to rest and recover. Owls roost in old buildings and trees, tarantula spiders return to their burrows, and mice huddle together in cosy nests. All keep very still, so that **predators** will not find them.

Bats live together in groups called **colonies**. In the daytime, a colony rests inside a cave, a tunnel or the roof of a building. There might be hundreds or thousands of bats hanging there, all resting together until night comes.

Did You Know?

Some night animals need a lot of sleep. The giant armadillo snoozes for eighteen hours a day.

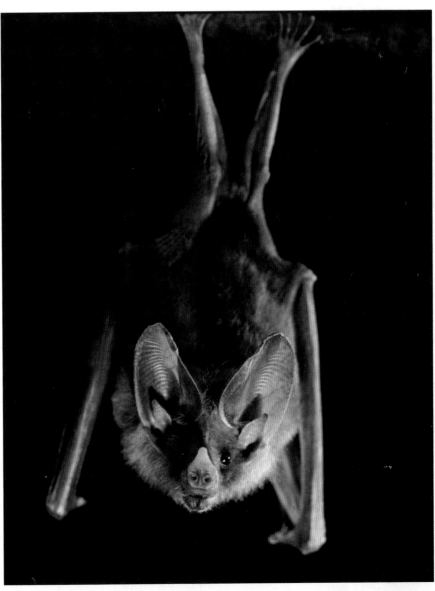

Long-eared bat

Why do big cats hunt at night?

Many big cats are nocturnal, including lions, tigers and leopards. They rest in the day, saving their energy until dark. At night, cats' eyes gather as much light as possible. Light enters through their large pupils, and is reflected off a layer at the back of the eye, called the **tapetum**. All cats have good night vision, and hunt at night when they can sneak up on their prey without being seen.

Serval

The serval is a small cat with a big bite. It is most active at dawn and dusk, but some are wide awake at night. It hunts rats, hares, snakes and lizards.

At night the Indian or Bengal tiger hunts wild boar, water buffalo, deer and monkeys. It creeps up on its prey, pounces on it, drags it to the ground, then kills it with a bite to the neck.

Indian tiger

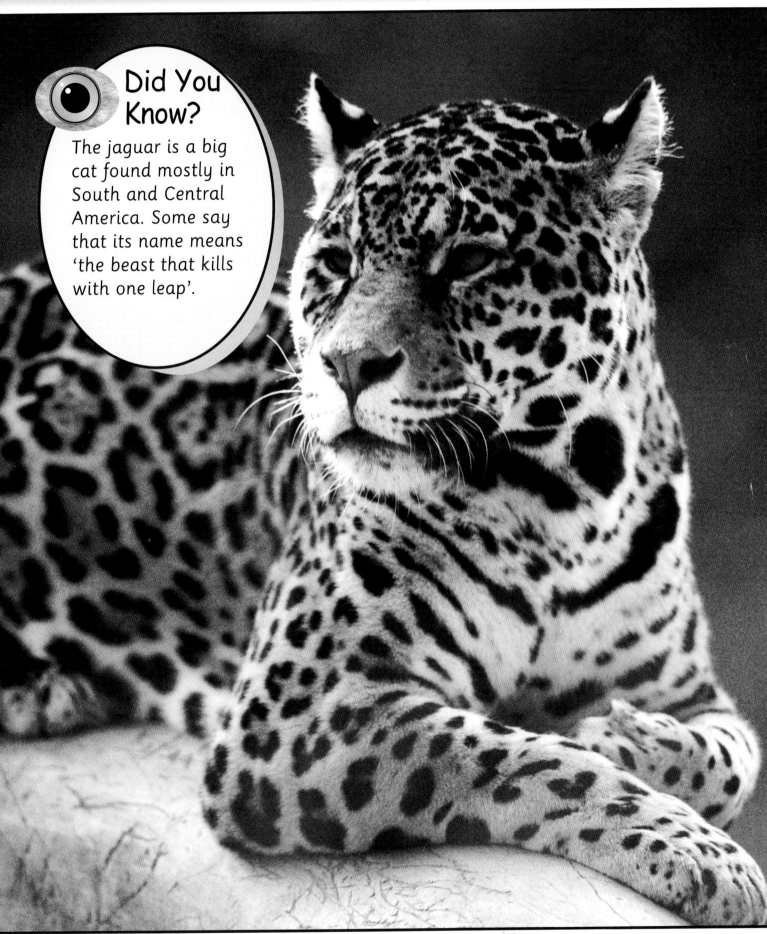

Did You Know?

The jaguar is a big cat found mostly in South and Central America. Some say that its name means 'the beast that kills with one leap'.

Jaguar

What lives in the rainforest at night?

Tropical rainforests around the world are home to a great variety of night animals. When darkness arrives, they emerge from their daytime resting places. Snakes slither in silence, insects crawl and fly, and mammals creep and leap. Night-time is their active period – and the most dangerous time for them. As they search for food, their movements give them away. If a predator is watching, the hunter becomes the hunted!

Green tree python

Lar gibbon

The Indian python is a massive snake from the tropical forests of Asia. A fully grown adult can be 6 metres long. At night it ambushes birds and mammals, wraps itself around them, and suffocates them until they are dead. Then it swallows them whole.

Indian python

The bigger the prey, the longer it takes the python to digest it. This gibbon will take a month to break down inside the python's stomach.

Hercules moth

These night animals live in the tropical rainforests of New Guinea and Australia.

Goodfellow's tree kangaroo

Did You Know?

The sugar glider is a possum which has a **membrane** of skin between its fingers and toes. When it jumps from a tree, it spreads out the membrane and can glide for up to 50 metres before landing in another tree.

Sugar glider

What senses are useful at night?

Many nocturnal animals have highly developed senses of sight and hearing. Unlike **diurnal** (daytime) animals, nocturnal animals such as cats and owls can see well at night.

Some bats use hearing to find prey. They make high-pitched sounds, which bounce off flying insects. Bats hear the echoes and know where to find the prey. This is called **echolocation**.

Eurasian owl

At the back of an owl's eyes, the shiny layer called the tapetum works like a mirror. It reflects the faintest traces of light back into the owl's eyes, giving the owl keen sight at night.

It's good to have big eyes. The bigger they are, the better they are for seeing at night, because they let more light in. At night the slow loris looks for insects to eat.

Slow loris

X-Ray Vision

Hold the next page up to the light to see the skeleton of the flying bat.

See what's inside

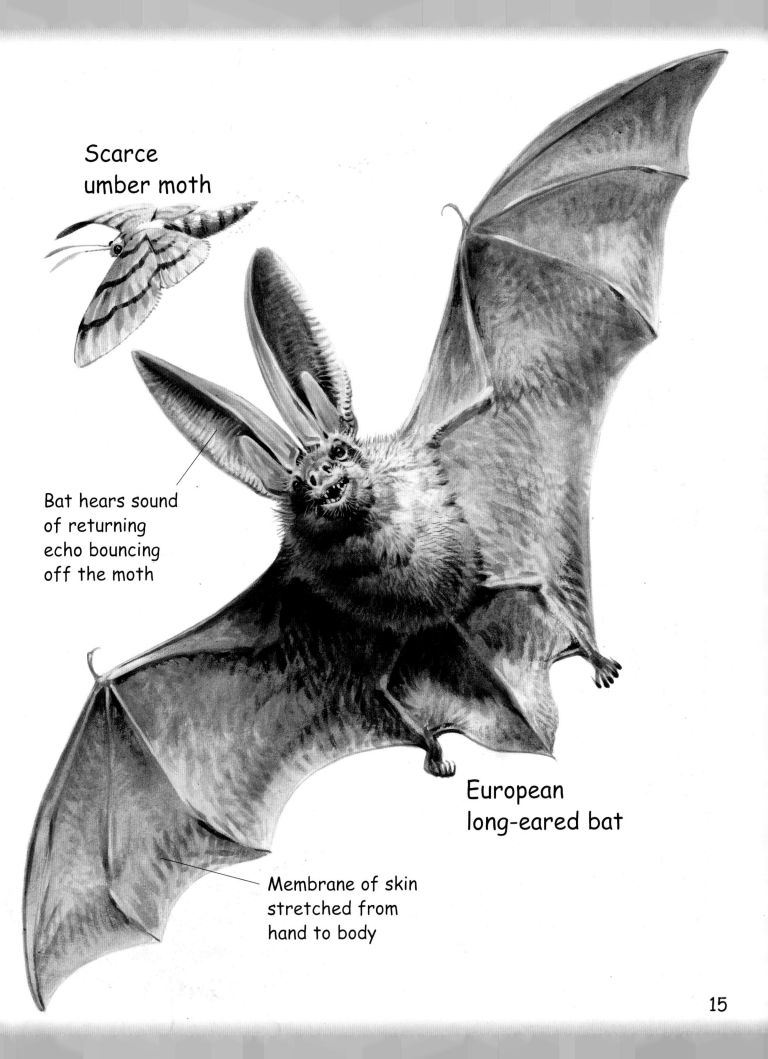

Scarce
umber moth

Bat hears sound
of returning
echo bouncing
off the moth

European
long-eared bat

Membrane of skin
stretched from
hand to body

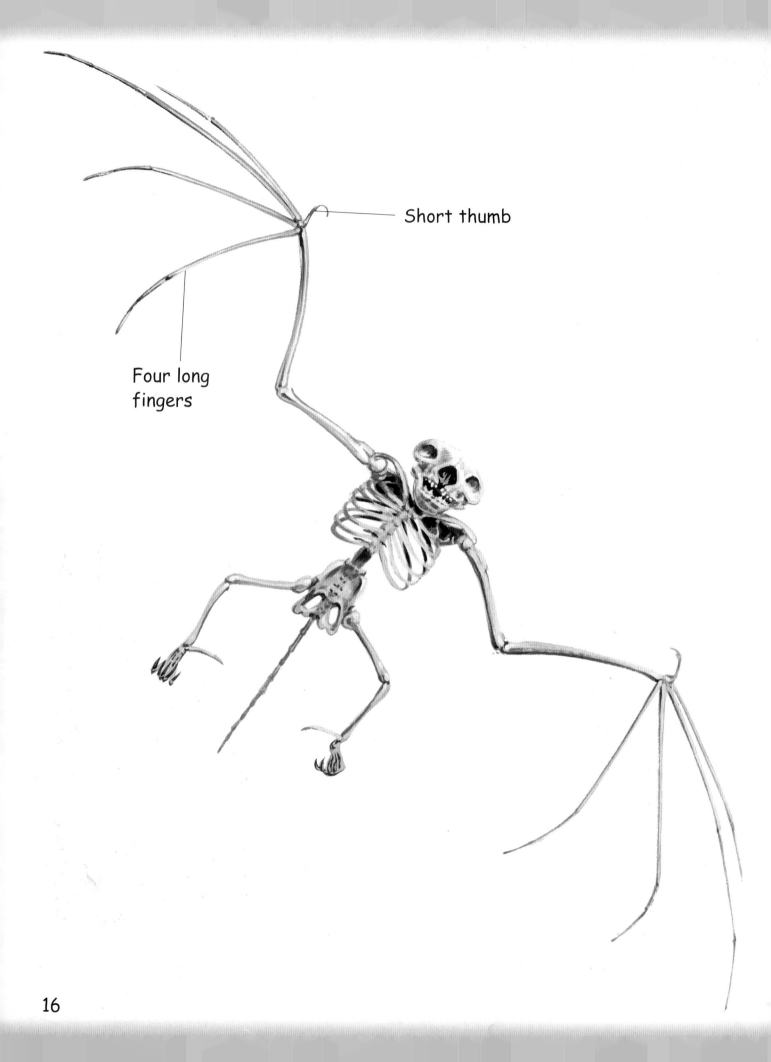

Short thumb

Four long
fingers

Fringe-lipped bat

Fringe-lipped bats of Central and South America don't use echolocation to find the frogs they eat. At night, they listen for croaking frogs, then swoop down and grab their meal. They are clever enough to tell the difference between the croaks of poisonous and non-poisonous frogs.

Do bats suck blood?

There are about one thousand different kinds of bats in the world. About two-thirds of all bats eat insects, and most others eat fruit, pollen and **nectar**. However, there is one bat family that doesn't eat insects or fruit. Instead, the vampire bats of South America feed on blood. At night, they land on cows or horses and bite through their skin. But vampire bats do not *suck* blood; they lick the flowing blood with their tongues.

Fruit bat

Why do sea turtles come onto land?

The green turtle spends most of its time swimming in the ocean. It's a big animal, and its flippers are designed for moving through water. But on land, these flippers are put to other uses. Females crawl onto sandy beaches at night, and slowly haul themselves above the high-tide mark. Then, in a safe place, they use their back flippers to dig a deep hole in the sand. It's a nest, where more than 100 eggs are laid. The turtle covers her nest with sand, then returns to the sea.

Female green turtle

Did You Know?

Green turtles have a good sense of direction. They will often lay their eggs on the same beach where they themselves were born, many years before.

Ghost crabs and frigate birds attack the baby turtles

The baby turtles hatch from their eggs after about 60 days. They hatch at night, and crawl straight to the sea. Crabs and gulls attack them on the beach, and sharks and dolphins eat them in the water.

When a green turtle hatches from its egg it is only about 50 mm long. If it survives the dangerous walk to the sea – and if it escapes from the ocean's predators – it can expect to grow to 1.5 metres long, and weigh about 135 kg. It might live for 80 years, and females will lay thousands of eggs in their lifetime.

Green turtle **hatchling**

What lurks at the bottom of the sea?

The seabed is the daytime resting place of the angel shark. It lives in most oceans, hiding at the bottom of the sea under a layer of mud or sand. Only its bulging eyes poke above the seabed. The angel shark is an ambush predator. At night, it watches for squid and fish to come within grabbing distance. It jumps up, sucks in, swallows, then settles back to lurk again.

Angel shark's eye

The angel shark's eyes are very sensitive to light. Shiny tapetum cells inside its eyes make dim light seem bright, helping it to see clearly in the dark.

White-tip reef sharks

Like the angel shark, the white-tip reef shark is a night-time feeder that dwells near the bottom of the sea. Found in the Indian and Pacific oceans, it rests throughout the day, hardly moving at all. When night arrives, it becomes active and starts to search for food.

The angel shark has a flat head and body. Its fins are large and wide. When it rests on the seabed it is almost invisible, because its colour and speckles act as **camouflage** against the sand.

Angel shark

White-tip reef sharks are the wolves of the sea. They hunt in large numbers, exploring crevices, holes and caves in search of prey such as octopus, lobsters, crabs, eels and other fish.

Why do owls spin their heads?

Most birds have eyes on the sides of their heads. This gives them all-round vision. Owls, though, have eyes at the front, and can only see straight ahead. If they want to see to the side or behind, they must turn their heads. Owls can spin their heads in almost a full circle without moving their bodies.

When an owl sits on a branch, it keeps very still. It has an excellent sense of hearing, and when it hears a movement it turns its head to have a look. Because it doesn't turn its body at the same time, it doesn't draw attention to itself, so its prey isn't scared away.

Pair of barn owls

Did You Know?

The great horned owl does not have horns – and the long-eared owl does not have long ears, either! The long tufts on their heads are feathers that just happen to look like horns or ears.

Great horned owl

What happens in deserts at night?

The world's sandy deserts are some of the hottest places on the planet. In the Sahara Desert, in Africa, temperatures reach a sweltering 50 degrees Celsius during the day. It's too hot to be out in such extreme heat, so many desert animals rest in burrows and other sheltered places. At night, when the temperature is cooler, they emerge from their dens and shelters. They are then active in the hours of darkness.

Desert scorpion

Scorpions are desert predators that ambush their prey at night. They can sense movements in the dark, then grab beetles, spiders and centipedes in their pincers.

Scorpions seek shade during the day

Oasis

Did You Know?

A kangaroo rat can live its whole life without drinking a drop of liquid. All of the water it needs comes from the seeds it eats.

The fennec fox is the smallest member of the fox family, and like other foxes it is nocturnal. It lives in northern Africa, where it hunts rodents, insects, lizards and birds. The fennec has very large ears, which have a double purpose. At night they listen out for prey, and in the day they help keep the fox cool by giving off body heat.

Fennec fox

Nocturnal animals that live in hot deserts have adapted to their harsh environment. They have learnt how to survive with little or no water. Desert mammals are often a light colour, which reflects heat and keeps them cool.

Gecko

Jerboa

Kangaroo rat

Could dinosaurs see at night?

Scientists think some dinosaurs were more active at night than in the daytime. Troodon,* a meat-eating dinosaur that lived near the North Pole, and Leaellynasaura,** a plant-eater that lived near the South Pole, had bigger eyes than most dinosaurs. Since they lived in places where nights were long and dark, night vision would have been essential to their survival.

* pronounced 'TRO-a-don'
** 'lee-ell-in-a-SORE-a'

Curled up tightly inside its egg is a baby Troodon. Adult Troodons grew to about 2 metres long, with eyes about 50 mm across. Troodon was a slender dinosaur that walked and ran on its two back legs. A **carnivore**, it preyed on smaller reptiles and mammals.

Inside a Troodon egg

Troodon

Saurornithoides

Troodon's eyes faced slightly forwards, which is typical of animals that hunt at night. This helped it to judge distances, allowing it to pounce on its prey.

27

Why do creepy crawlies come out at night?

Night-time is the best time for moths, spiders and many kinds of insects, as there are fewer predators around to trouble them. If they came out in the day, they would be eaten by birds, frogs and lizards. Under cover of darkness, moths sip nectar from flowers, other insects forage for food, and spiders wait for prey. Their senses work best at night, especially their sense of smell, which helps them sniff out food.

Cockroaches

Cockroaches hide during the day. At night they emerge in large numbers, and will eat just about anything.

Tarantula fangs

The Mexican red-kneed tarantula is a large, hairy spider from Central and South America. It lives in a burrow during the day. At night it waits by the entrance for passing insects, millipedes, scorpions and other spiders. It jumps on its prey, killing it by injecting it with poison through its fangs.

Mexican red-kneed tarantula

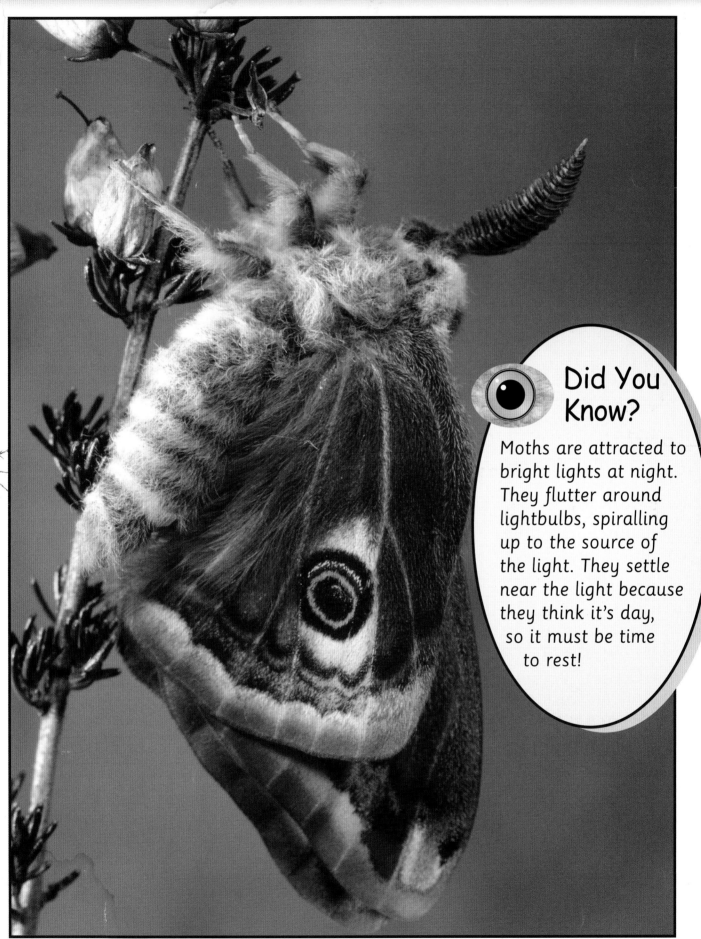

Did You Know?

Moths are attracted to bright lights at night. They flutter around lightbulbs, spiralling up to the source of the light. They settle near the light because they think it's day, so it must be time to rest!

Emperor moth

Night creature facts

Aye-aye

The aye-aye, from Madagascar, is the world's largest nocturnal primate. It eats grubs that live inside trees. To find a grub, it taps on a tree trunk and listens for a hollow sound. Then it bites into the hollow, pokes its long, thin middle finger into the space, and picks out a fat, juicy grub.

The colour of an owl's eyes indicates its hunting time. Yellow eyes show that it is a diurnal (daytime) hunter. Owls with orange eyes are crepuscular (dawn and dusk) hunters, while night-time (nocturnal) owls have dark eyes.

The eyes of nocturnal animals see mostly rough outlines and little or no colour. They are big, to attract maximum light at night. An owl's eyes fill more than half of its skull.

In daylight, nocturnal animals such as lizards can narrow their pupils by squinting or closing their eyelids. This helps to keep bright light out of their sensitive eyes.

Twenty million Mexican free-tailed bats live in Bracken Cave, Texas, USA. They eat an estimated 250 tonnes of insects every night!

The venom of a Mexican red-kneed tarantula paralyses its prey and starts to dissolve it. Once the prey's insides have started to turn to liquid, the spider sucks it out, until all that is left is a hollow skin or a body case.

Asian leopard cat attacking a lesser tree shrew

Glossary

camouflage Special colouring that makes an animal difficult to see in its usual habitat.

carnivore A meat-eating animal.

colony A large family group of bats or other animals living together.

constriction Crushing; snakes that kill their prey by crushing are called **constrictors**.

crepuscular Active mostly in twilight, at dusk and dawn.

diurnal Active mostly during the day.

echolocation The method used by bats to detect their prey. They make high-pitched sounds and listen for these sounds as they bounce back off the prey.

habitat The kind of place in which an animal naturally prefers to live.

hatchling A newly hatched animal.

membrane A thin, tough layer of skin.

nectar A sugary substance produced by flowers to attract birds, bats and insects, which then help to pollinate the flowers.

nocturnal Active mostly at night.

predator Any animal that hunts and kills other animals for food.

prey Any animal that is killed and eaten by a predator.

tapetum (or **tapetum lucidum**) A layer of reflecting cells at the back of the eye of some animals. It helps them to see in the dark.

tropical Belonging to the tropics – the part of the earth furthest from the poles, where the temperature is always hot.

Mouse
opossum

Index